MATILDA KERRY

Life After an Autism Diagnosis

The Ultimate Guide to Home Proofing for your Autistic Child

This book was professionally typeset on Reedsy.
Find out more at reedsy.com

I dedicate this book to my wonderful family.
You all make every day so worth it!

"Holland?!?" you say. "What do you mean Holland?? I signed up for Italy! I'm supposed to be in Italy. All my life I've dreamed of going to Italy."

But there's been a change in the flight plan. They've landed in Holland and there you must stay.

... So you must go out and buy new guidebooks. And you must learn a whole new language...

A snippet from "Welcome to Holland"
by Emily Perl Kingsley

Contents

1

Introduction

"Your child has Autism!" Words out of a doctor's mouth, that no parent wants to hear, but you got it anyway. You feel shock, disbelief, and despair, followed by a set of why and how questions and self-blame. "How did this happen?" "Was it something you did while pregnant?", "Is it a family curse!?, "Does the Doctor even know what they're talking about?" The questions come in such a rush, you barely hear the Doctor explain key aspects of the Diagnosis - how your child might need support for the rest of their life, let alone the action plan for their management.

In my case, the doctor said, my son would require a moderate level of support throughout his life! "What did this even mean?" I had no clue.

Then comes the biggest question of them all - "What do I do now?" But unlike me who had practically no one to turn to, thankfully you have this guidebook, which is your first weapon in navigating the very confusing, very challenging, and very beautiful journey of raising a child with Autism.

I'm Matilda Kerry, a Proud Autism Mom to a seven-year-old son and a specialist public health Doctor. When I got my diagnosis, my world stopped, literally stopped for 3 days, I cannot account for what I did or what happened in those 3 days that followed the diagnosis, it is a complete blur for me, it was my mourning period a very critical and necessary part of your journey that we are going to cover in the first chapter of this book. But this guidebook is so much more than mourning and emerging with hope. This book will help you prep for a drastic change in your life, routine, and yes - home. These changes are necessary to build the skills your very special child needs to navigate a world that simply isn't built for them.

I'm not promising that at the end of this book, you will have all the knowledge needed to get your child communicating (maybe even talking!), socializing, and with little or no sensory seeking, but after you've read this book, you will have the knowledge and tools to enhance your home in a way that your child with Autism can communicate with you and those around him better and begin building skills for the larger world around them. This book is a pathway and opens the door to communication, language, fewer meltdowns, socialization and so much more. Let's begin!

2

How to use this book

My advice is to read this book at a stretch with an open mind. Don't even take notes at first, just read. I want you to be fully relaxed when you are reading because your mind is locking away the salient things that directly relate to you and your child and will bring them up again the second time you go through this book. That way you don't waste precious time jotting down things to home proof that you may not even need, or that your child would not respond to in a million years!

Time is of the essence, so I strongly advise you to get to it. The first five years of a child's life are the years when the brain is most malleable. You can really set the foundation for their success or lifelong struggle in this world. So find a quiet spot away from distractions and discover the immediate steps you need to take over the next few months to ensure your home becomes a stimulating environment for your autistic child, helping them to continually learn, make mistakes, adapt, socialize, connect, have fun, and experience his or her life.

This guidebook is not a stand-alone tool for providing home therapy to your Autistic child, this book should be used within a comprehensive therapy plan created by medical specialists in line with your child's medical diagnosis of Autism Spectrum Disorder.

3

Mourn

The right way to grieve

Is there a right way to grieve? Well, I think so! For me, I grieved from the doctor's office, all the way home, and for 3 days that followed. I was numb. I remember getting into the car, but the ride home was a blur. My ever-active son was doing his usual thing, just blabbing away in that world that was entirely his while he watched his favorite nursery rhymes on my android phone. I recall looking at him, and him appearing strange to me - "My strange boy..." I thought, "what am I to do with you?" Somehow, I got home and am still numb. Like a robot, I do all the usual chores I should do, thinking over and over - "How did I get here?" "What do I do now?"

It's evening somehow and my husband walks in.

"How did it go at the Doctor's office?" He asks casually."

"It went OK," I respond, "our son has Autism."

Frankly, I don't remember much after that, but I do remember being afraid of hearing myself say the "A" word - Autism - I remember the deep sinking fear, that began pulling me down into a deep abyss. At night I cried, the same way that I would usually cry when heartbroken - silently, biting into the pillow. I've always felt silly and vulnerable crying in front of others, so I don't. I put up a steely exterior when I'm hurt and find a quiet place to expel my grief, that's how I mourn, and I'm darn proud of it! I was in this state for 3 days before I began to feel any relief, before I began to seek resources to home proof for my son.

Why am I telling you this? Mourning is a very necessary step in getting your mind where it needs to be to begin addressing the world to function for your child, because your child is not the problem, the world is. From childhood, we've been conditioned to believe that typical is better, that disability is a curse, disability is hard to manage, ugly and not acceptable. Hence naturally when we get a disability diagnosis for our child or children we feel devastated and feel a loss. But it's not what it seems, trust me - there is so much you will gain over this journey. You will learn patience, organization and planning, child education, conflict resolution, and people management like no other. I know my journey has made me a better mum, employee, spouse, and person in general. Four years after my diagnosis I can tell you that I would not have it any other way. I was made to be an Autism mum, and everything is as it should be. Don't get me wrong, I'm not saying that there are no hard days, or days when I wish for a slower pace and less to do, I'm saying that everything you need to build your Autistic child is available all around you, you just have to have the right tools, like this book in your hands.

So, step one - Mourn! There are quiet mourners like me, there are those who mourn with anger and venting, some who need a shoulder to cry on, and many who become couch potatoes, watching everything and nothing as they consume bowl after bowl of their favorite ice cream. Whichever way you wish - Mourn. But have a time limit to it. Mine was 3 days, yours may be less or more, set a limit to this period even though it's a state that's hard to control. If you are sad, you are sad and only you can take deliberate actions to overcome grief. Be encouraged to, knowing that the sooner you recover from this phase and get to work on home-proofing for your Autistic child, the better for your child, their siblings, your spouse, friends, family, and everyone you are connected to. If you have trouble shaking off the blues post-diagnosis, you may be slipping into prolonged grief or depression, please contact a specialist for grief counseling if this becomes the case.

Clear your head

Clearing your head means finding a healthy outlet for all the fear, regret, and negative emotions that have built up since the diagnosis. This step kind of flows out from mourning. Here you are trying to get your mind as close to its pre-diagnosis state, that's assuming you were in a good place to start with. You require a lot of encouragement and hope to clear your head. This may come in the form of family support, online articles, poems, religious messages, or practical guides, to give yourself a sense of "I am not alone!", "I have support!", and "I can do this!". If you have a supportive family, they can be very instrumental in helping you clear your head and get in the right state of mind to act. Sadly, in my case, my family was more terrified than I was about the diagnosis and quickly adopted the denial route.

I remember a friend looking me straight in the eyes and saying, "It's not your son that has Autism, it's you!" She was so mad at me and at my audacity for accepting the diagnosis which to her was worse than a curse! If the situation hadn't been so serious I would have laughed at the ridiculousness of the moment. I mean I'm his mother, I should be more upset about the diagnosis than her, right? Anyways we'll cover more about - telling others about the diagnosis, in the next section of this book.

For me clearing my head took a lot of connecting with online stories of mums like myself. So, I'd just sit for hours soaking up encouraging, triumphant stories of mums bringing up their children with autism. I also started a blog that held all my thoughts and feelings - it was the ultimate outlet for all my negative pent-up emotions. I count myself extremely lucky to have found the poem - Welcome to Holland, by Emily Perl Kingsley. I highly recommend every Autism-Parent read this poem, it was the start and end of my mourning, and I pray it is for you too.

Another thing I did to clear my head was to get back into an exercise routine. Exercise for me was about detoxing, ridding my body in line with my mind of all the negatives. It was extremely helpful because when you exercise, you feel good. So, I went back to yoga, which is low-stress and has the added advantage of calming the mind and spirit. I also got my sister on board so there was a higher likelihood of sticking to the routine. My yoga time was my time and my escape from everything including the uncertainty of Autism. Doing something for yourself and yourself alone can help you not to feel overwhelmed by the whole situation and to remember that there are other priorities, joys, and things to engage in.

Home proofing for family and friends

Now telling your spouse about the diagnosis is a must-do, you need each other to get through this, and if you team up, the chances are better for your Autistic child to build needed skills. However, this is rarely the case as opposing beliefs and different coping mechanisms between spouses usually lead to clashes and more stress in the home. For me, my spouse took longer, more, specifically 2 years longer than I did to believe the diagnosis and get with the program. But at least he stuck around, and he got there, and now I have his support in building the mechanisms and structures our son needs. However, some spouses may react worse. Sometimes spouses either the husband or wife cannot cope with the pressure and leave the other spouse to figure things out. You must be prepared for the worst-case scenario, at the same time, you should give your spouse time to mourn and clear their heads as you did.

Men are again conditioned by the world to be tough and not break down in tears with grief, so women may find their feet faster and forge ahead of their male partners. Whatever the case the stronger partner should have empathy towards the weaker and instead of being critical redirect energies to demonstrating the impact that home-proofing interventions are having on your child's communication, language, behavior, social skills, and general growth. Once your spouse sees it working, they will get with the program (if they are smart and truly love you and your child). So, it doesn't matter how long, as long as they get there. In the meantime, redirect your energies to your child and your plan for them.

With friends and family sharing the diagnosis is kind of a "damned if you do, damned if you don't" scenario because both have their downsides. If you don't tell family and close friends, you'd have to keep hiding the truth from them and that takes effort and energy that you frankly should be spending helping your child, not even considering the damage and toll this path will take on your mental health and emotions. Anxiety will be the tale of the day as you wonder if your child will cause a scene at the next birthday party, when you run into a friend at the mall, or when a friend calls unannounced at your home. It was just too much uncertainty for me to even consider this path, I could not bring myself to hide my sunshine under a pot plant, my son is just too bright and smart and cute and loving to hide. Yes, he could burst a meltdown at the slightest notice and didn't have enough words to communicate his basic needs at age 3, - that didn't change anything! I am so proud of him and his budding abilities. I have never been and am not ashamed of my son, he is perfect and I don't care what other people think, knowing he's autistic, this is MY journey.

However many may struggle to share this information and you are not obliged to. Sharing also comes with its problems, like the torrent of questions and resurfacing of fear and self-doubt. "What are you going to do now?" "Have you tried this and that? "Did you take him for prayers and spiritual deliverance?" "Maybe the diagnosis is wrong!" "I don't see anything wrong with him, he's just acting silly, he's just a slow talker." There is nothing you won't hear, so stay strong and appear strong and in control even if you may not feel so. Doubt breeds more doubt and panic.

I would say in all that there is really no right or wrong way to tell the family about your child, or if to do so in the first place. I wouldn't advise you to present it in memo form or as a part of your to-do list, it should naturally happen. Friends, if truly close to you, should have already had some insight into your concerns about your child, so sharing the diagnosis should be like a continuing conversation rather than a fresh one. With friends you aren't very close to you, a situation would no doubt present itself for you to share if you feel so inclined, there is no need to make the rounds telling everyone. I'd give an example - One time, a not-too-close friend of mine came to visit, and she noticed some communication visuals around my home, out of curiosity she asked, "Who are these for, is it for teaching the kids?", to which I replied that the visuals were for my son, explaining further that he had some communication difficulty due to Autism. She was surprised and went on to say she had never thought anything to be wrong with my son, (which there isn't, but hey, that was a conversation for another day, pick your battles....), she then went on to encourage me to pray and that was that. However, over the next few visits - mine to hers and hers to mine, I noticed she always made her older son kind of mentor mine. He would model good behavior and teach him, age-appropriate responsibilities, like clearing the table and cleaning up toys after playtime. I thought that was great and loved the added socialization opportunities it presented. Now that kind of friend is a keeper and welcome in my home! Yes, you must home-proof for friends and family too.

Now, some family and some friends will support you, they will become your rock, however, some will only be full of bad advice, discouragement, denial, and fear which are downright unhelpful to you right now. The decision here then becomes simple - Keep supportive people around you and un-supportive people as far away as possible. Tough times call for tough decisions and measures. Be unapologetic about yours at this time.

Reconnect with your child

When I got my diagnosis, my boy immediately felt strange to me, this was because I was paralyzed with fear i felt unprepared and unequipped, with a herculean task dropped in my lap.

Feeling disconnected from your child after being told they have a disability is not out of place, although some may feel this to a higher degree than others. I remember how I would sometimes look at him and internally shake my head in denial, the things I previously thought were cute like him repeating the same motion with his hands began to bother me, and I became harsher towards him in some ways because I wanted..., no needed him to change, and to change immediately so society would accept him and not ostracize him. I didn't want my son to be judged or to endure any humiliation or pain. Many parents make this mistake after a diagnosis, getting immediately caught up in fixing their child that they disconnect from the nurture aspect of parenting. Be careful about this - the aim of home-proofing is not to fix your child but to help build skills that allow them to function in the world around them and hopefully gain independence.

I had to do some serious self-reflection to realize I was going down this path, I had to find a way out and back to the son I loved so very deeply and still did but had somehow lost my way. So what did I do to reconnect?

1. I revisited old memories, the most loving ones. I would deliberately think back to my most precious moments with my son. His birth, his first word (which was "pap" a Nigerian baby cereal he didn't like to eat!), his christening, his first birthday, him pointing to the sky at 2 years and saying "moon". Meeting him and my mum at the airport after weeks away from him to study...., I looked back at photos that made my heart swell.

2. I made deliberate physical contact, hugging and kissing him all day long for no reason at all, other than just because he was all mine!

3. I coined special names for him "My Champ", "Papi", and "My daddy!" Names that built confidence in him and me as well.

4. I took out days where just he and I would go out and just do us. We'd go to play zones, as he loved the ball pit, and I'd watch him play. Sometimes we'd just stroll around the neighborhood and I'd point out things to him like the sky, birds, stones, plants, and flowers. He loved picking flowers on the way back home from my neighbor's front yard.

Re-connection is a process, a deliberate process that I worked hard on, and one day I was back right where I had left off and have since gone beyond that in the depth of love that I have for my son. A mother's love never dies, we are mum, mommy, mother, and the love and connection are so powerful and eternal! Fathers too have a special connection with their children this should be nurtured in the same way. If you are feeling disconnected from your child right now, don't feel alone or ashamed about it, again your mind, heart, and soul are recovering from the shock of the news you've received, and will take time to recover. You love your child, unconditionally, nothing will change this, even though you may not be feeling it as much these days. Take deliberate actions as I did to reconnect. Reopen your heart - find warmth and healing. Reconnection is about acceptance and you must accept your child for who they are to make any meaningful impact on their progress.

Mourn - Advice Summary

1. Grieve the way you usually do. You've been conditioned to believe you've lost something and your mind, soul, and

body need to recover from this shock

2. Subconsciously set a time frame to feel loss, seek encouragement, and move on

3. If you find it hard to shake off the blues after a week, see professional help.

4. Find encouragement by connecting with stories, groups, or families with children with disabilities

5. Find a positive outlet for your fears, regret, sadness, and loss. Consider writing or saying how you feel and what you hope for, in a recording, or just out loud in an empty room. You do not have to start a blog and you do not have to share what you write or say with others

6. Read "Welcome to Holland" by Emily Perl Kingsley

7. Detox – Clearing your body also helps clear your mind, so exercise, eat well, and drink plenty of water

8. If you are the stronger spouse, give your partner time to mourn and recover, if they are un-supportive for a long time, channel your energies to your child's progress. Your spouse will watch, learn, and get with the program

9. If you feel you haven't been the most supportive spouse after reading this book it's not too late to pick up the slack and be more supportive of your spouse and efforts geared towards the well-being of your child. Bring some tips from this book to the table and get in the game!

10. The decision to tell family and friends and the time to do so is entirely up to you – I advise telling family and friends when you've cleared your head and are paving a path to your next action steps, unless they are part of your mourning phase, like a dependable family or friend's shoulder to cry on.

11. Tell friends when the opportunity arises, and not as a

deliberate effort. Let them know your plans and that you'd appreciate their support and not sympathy. Allow them time to process, and observe your true friends stick around.

12. Keep supportive friends close, the latter go in the litter
13. Don't beat yourself up about not feeling connected with your child, give it time
14. Look at baby photos, transitioning up until the current stage, and be deliberate in demonstrating affection to your child - cuddle them, kiss them whether the situation warrants it or not. Do things they enjoy with them - tickles, piggyback rides, tummy bubbles, bike rides outside, strolls and have special "us" days - go to the park, movies, play zone, supermarket, zoo, wherever your child feels safe, is least likely to throw a tantrum, and where you can both share moments.

4

Plan

Understand the Diagnosis

Understanding your child's diagnosis is the most important step in home proofing and I say this because this is what is going to guide all the modifications you make in your home. To put things simply, you want to understand your child's strengths and challenges so you can tailor and build solutions in the place he spends the most time - which is your home. You also have to get your "home team" assembled if you are lucky to have one, speaking of - your supportive spouse, a sibling, or other caregivers in the home (grandma, grandpa, aunties, nannies, etc.) In understanding the diagnosis, carry your home team along so they can always support your efforts, and to understand the diagnosis is not to research the nuances and theories behind Autism or the medical jargon shared in the diagnostic report. No, not even I as a doctor concern myself much with the theory of why or how autism happens, because I quickly discovered that Autism spectrum disorder still carries a huge question mark and a lot is still being uncovered about the condition. I decided to leave the research community to do their job, researching the genesis and cures if any, while I directed my energies within my space of influence - to build my child's competencies to a stage where he is in no way disadvantaged.

I strongly advise you get your diagnosis from an expert - usually a developmental pediatrician, community Pediatrician, or public health physician. The diagnosis is usually performed by a multidisciplinary team led by the pediatrician (or public health physician) and comprised of the speech therapist, child psychologist, occupational therapist, physiotherapist, etc, who each review the child using specific assessment tools and combine findings for a final diagnosis. An individual doctor isn't going to examine your child and just come up with a diagnosis of Autism, if that's what you got, I'd strongly query the diagnosis and seek a second opinion. The diagnostic report in your hands should cover your child's areas of strengths and challenges across the developmental domains as well as give recommendations and a plan of action. Again I'm blessed to have had and still have access to one of the best service centers for children with Autism in Nigeria - The Children's Developmental Center. They provided the highest quality diagnosis, recommendations, and guidance. From the diagnostic report, a 30 pager, which I've read back to back over a hundred times, clearly pinpointed his strengths - Motor, cognition, (reading, spelling, memory, recall) and challenges - eye contact, cognition (executive functioning skills) communicating needs, fine motor, etc. It was based on this that I started to build a resilient home for my son. I will try to make this easy by breaking the developmental domains into six, I've also included physical health as a domain. Read your child's diagnosis and try to group their strengths and difficulties in the categories below using the sample table to expand on the findings.

1. Communication – expressive and receptive language
2. Gross motor – walking, running, jumping
3. Fine motor – writing, pinching, stringing, eating with cutlery
4. Sensory – hearing, sight, skin sensation
5. Behavior – stimming, meltdowns, OCD
6. Cognition – Understanding concepts, feelings, academics
7. Physical Health – food fads, picky eaters, immunity, mental health, co-morbidities (hearing, visual impairments)

Table 1 – Strengths and Challenges

Domain	Strength	Challenges
Communication	Can point and take an adult to what they need	Cannot express wants and needs verbally
Gross motor	Appropriate for age e.g. Can sit up straight, walk, run, jump	Nil
Fine motor	Can eat with a spoon	Difficulty holding a pencil, pinching pegs
Social skills	Imaginative play	Poor eye contact
SensorY	Good eyesight, good hearing	Hypersensitivity to sound and light
Behavior	Listens to instructions, responds to prompts	Head banging
Cognition	Memory, recall, spelling, reading	Does not understand emotions
Physical Health	No additional impairments - e.g Visual or hearing	Bowel problems - abdominal pain, constipation, diarrhea Malnutrition from restricted diets Recurrent upper respiratory tract infections Recurrent mouth ulcers

My final advice at this juncture is to get someone else, e.g. your spouse or another physician, to read the diagnostic report and tell you what they understand and make of it, or give advice, and here's why. As explained in chapter one, I had heard autism at the diagnosis and hadn't heard anything else as my soul plunged into darkness, I had then gone on to read the report focusing on only Autism which had been branded into the back of my mind, and even though I honestly cannot count the number of times I've re-read my son's report I completely missed his sub-diagnosis of Attention deficit hyperactive disorder (ADHD). It wasn't until 1 year after on a follow-up report that I saw and registered this! Already a year had passed without any home intervention for ADHD. A second pair of trusted eyes would catch anything salient you might have missed

Translating your diagnosis into a plan

After completing the "strengths and challenges" exercise, the next step is to prioritize the skills you want to see grow first. Prioritize these skills across the domains so you don't leave any core area out, and I know you want to tackle everything all at once, I really sympathize with you because I was once there! However, that's not just possible. Remember this is a lifelong journey and that this book is just helping with a very minute but significant aspect of it - baby steps.

When you've prioritized, please know this, it's so important and will guide your follow-up decisions. Although I discovered this a bit later in my journey, my son was already 6 years old, it's guided my recent home-proofing decisions better. I read a featured article by Temple Grandin, who is Autistic and has a Ph.D. in Animal Science, (she is so awesome!) which theorized that people with autism think in specific details. The detail type they use is very specialized and often rigid (but not always). There are autistic people who think in pictures (visual learners), those who think in patterns (great in music, math, and puzzles), and those who are verbal thinkers (great recall of facts and trivia, good at learning languages, etc.) Lucky for me, even before this knowledge, I had somehow deciphered that my son remembered things better if he had seen pictures, especially different picture representations of that item. So visuals had become a huge part of my son's daily exposure. Everything I could present to him in pictures, I did, physically, through a computer, or in printed form, laminated, and cut out. if I had prior knowledge about thinking specializations I would have introduced some verbal logic aids, as my son also thinks in this way sometimes. It's not too late though, as I've started doing this. The trick is not to give up and to keep researching and introducing new things, children are always learning and developing right up into adulthood - as an adult I'm still learning and so are you.

Now armed with your child's strengths and challenges, and hopefully, insight into how they think, your immediate priority is to get them communicating with you and the world. I said communicating and not talking because some people with Autism remain nonverbal or minimally verbal all their lives - set your expectations realistically and prioritize giving your child a way to communicate. Communication goes beyond speaking a language, it can be through text apps, Picture Exchange Communication (PECS), sign language, or a combination of all these. Fortunately, in the course of building communication, language often does emerge, if so you would have accomplished 2 victories, that being said, your focus should be on communication. This is your first and most important task because the sooner your child can communicate their needs, the less frustrated they are, the calmer they are and the less their challenging behaviors become. These two books - "Carly's Voice" by Arthur Fleischmann and Carly Fleischmann and "How to Talk if my lips don't Move" by Tito Rajarshi Mukhopadhyay can help parents of nonverbal kids find inspiration and practical ways to support their child's communication.

So what kind of visuals do you need:

● schedules - that guide the flow of the day from waking up, to bath, meal time, playtime, potty time, evening entertainment, bedtime, etc

● food choices - small cut-out pictures or fully laminated pictures of food items - apple, banana, bread, milk, eggs, etc

● Behaviors and Emotions - emojis or real people's faces to help understand feelings

● Event sequences - First, then or Now, later, etc

● Instructions - wait, go, sit, stand, sleep, etc

● Clothing items - Shirt, shorts, dress, hat, belt, gloves, etc

I advise having the word written under each picture, this way you are building on their comprehension, communication, and word recognition skills at the same time. For more details on visuals in each category, visit the Autism speaks link in resources which has further instructions and resource websites for how to make and use your visuals at home. It's a great place to start! When you've prioritized action areas, you are ready to begin building resources and shaping the space around your home to deliver on the task at hand.

Set short and long-term goals

Pulling from your prioritized action areas, set simple short and long-term goals. I remember using developmental milestones as a yardstick for my short and long-term goals. When my son was three, he had about 50 words in his vocabulary, although he wasn't using them all to communicate, he could identify the words and sometimes say them in the right context.

My short-term goal would have been something along these lines:

By age 4, be able to speak in 4-5 word sentences and use most words in the right context.

Or

By age 5 my daughter should be able to request all her needs using picture exchange communication and single words.

Set realistic goals right, wrong! I say set your goals in line with what you want to see both short-term and long-term and go for it. You may not reach these goals within your desired time frame but having goals means you are always striving for more and hence supporting your child to build skills.

Long-term goals for me are like the ultimate vision for my son in the future. It may go like this:

My child can communicate with me, family, peers, and the community enough to build and maintain good relationships.

Think through and write down your goals, they are road maps you can refer back to, to see where you started and how far you've come. We started from a point of 50 words in the vocabulary and one-word requests to get needs met, now we have thousands of words and 4-5 word requests (most of the time at least!), and attempts at conversation. It's possible, set those goals!

PLAN - Advice Summary:

1. Get your diagnosis from a specialist team
2. Read and re-read the diagnostic report until you under-

stand it

3. Sieve out your child's strengths and difficulties as per the diagnostic report
4. Get a 2nd pair of eyes on the report to identify additional action areas
5. Discuss ambiguous areas of the report with your managing physician or therapist
6. Inform your home team and ensure understanding at each member level
7. Aim high for your short-term goals, and extend them into the long-term goal
8. Write down your short and long-term goals, they are road maps for tracking how far you've come

5

Let's have fun - Shop!

What to buy and ditch

Yes, there's some fun and excitement when it comes to shopping for my son, and I'm not talking about clothes, shoes, or toys. I'm talking about learning tools! However, before you go all out and began to acquire tools and devices you may never use, I advise you to start home-proofing small and build up over months and years. Why? Well, your child is constantly growing, needs change, they may not gravitate or respond to the tools you get because they aren't ready for it yet, or it's just not their thing. Also going on the internet and buying every tool or toolbox for Autism (as there are plenty on the market) is not the best approach. Show inline with your prioritized areas for action. For each priority, start by deciding on one tool to introduce at home in addition to his other therapies, deciding on tools requires a lot of research.

When I first started home proofing, I didn't even realize I was doing this. It was something that naturally happened as I worked to support my son build needed skills. Language was a priority area, he was minimally verbal and I was working to get him fully verbal. I knew I needed a speech therapist, but they were scarce in Nigeria, so I search for speech therapy substitutes online and after many days, I found Video modeling specifically a program called Gemiini Systems which applies evidence-based discrete video modeling through an online platform to teach language, communication, social and behavior skills. Of course, 1st on my shopping list was a tablet compatible with the Gemiini app and 24 hours Wi-Fi. This was my home-proofing intervention for the speech domain.

This is how you should build your shopping list. Look at the area you want to build and decide based on research, on tools for that specific task. My rule of thumb is to use a tool for at least 6 months before deciding they don't work. Once you are sure they aren't working (at least not for now) place them in storage, it may become handy one day. I recall buying a fidget spinner for my son when he was 4 years old as a sensory-calming tool, but he never used it or seemed interested in it. So I simply threw it out. A few weeks back, 3 years later, he asked me for a fidget spinner after seeing it on the internet, skeptically I bought it, and he's been using it to keep his hands busy. This was a huge lesson for me. If it doesn't work now, it doesn't mean it's not going to work in a few months or years down the line.

I've listed some of the most helpful tools I have used and still use to date to home-proof. This list is limited, you'd still have to do some research in line with your child's specific needs. Remember to start small and build up. Buy one or two items with a plan and approach for the area of work in mind.

Table 2 - Shopping List

Domain	Tools
Communication	Tools for creating visuals - Paper, printer, lamination equipment, scissors, Velcro, two-way sticky tapes, reusable adhesive e.g blue tack Access to Picture exchange communication system (PECS), Tablet, Wi-Fi, speech therapy apps
Gross motor	Crawl tunnel, trampoline, pull ropes, Proprioception tools - yoga ball, body pods, balance pods and beams, indoor and outdoor stepping stones, therapy swing
Fine motor	Play dough, tweezers, pencil grips, stringing toys, grippable cutlery set, stacker toys
Social skills	Character toys (community workers), bubble toys, turn-taking games
Sensory	Bean chair, chew toys, fidget spinners, pop-ins, z-vibe brush, body brush, sensory toys, sensory ball, weighted blanket, weighted jackets, noise canceling headset
Behavior	Timer, visual schedules, emotion literacy charts, calming technique visuals
Cognition	Flashcards, Sequence cards, learning apps, class-appropriate textbooks and workbooks, pencils, erasers, colored markers, coloring paint, counters, abacus, puzzles
Physical Health	Healthy meal plan Medicine cabinet with over counter meds for colds, pains, multivitamins, Omega 3, docosahexaenoic acid (DHA), Probiotics, etc. First Aid box Assistive technology for any co-morbidity e.g. Magnifiers, hearing aid

Shopping list sample

Amy is 3 years old and needs the following areas of work addressed – Behavior (head banging), Sensory (oral sensitivities – chews on items), Communication (difficulty communicating needs)

1. Behavior – Head protection helmet
2. Sensory – Chew toy
3. Communication difficulty – tools to create visuals of food items i.e. paper, printer, lamination tool, scissors, access to PECS pictures, Wi-Fi

SHOP – Advice Summary

1. Don't go out on a whim and buy all that you feel would be

useful, have an approach, and tools in mind
2. Start small and build up over months and years
3. Make a shopping list starting with one item for each domain of focus
4. Some tools will work now, and some would work later, if it does have the desired effect, Shelf it, don't trash it

6

It's time to build

Be Prepared

Take a deep breath and brace yourself, in a bid to home-proof for your child's needs, there would need to be some degree of remodeling and additions to your maybe serene environment, things may start to appear tacky, but hey! That's completely ok, you child over ambiance, every time! Home proofing was a gradual process that took many years for me - four to be precise, and I am not done yet, I don't think I will ever be done, because my son is growing, changing, and developing, and so are the tools required to meet his needs. Some things he's grown out of completely, like the sensory brush we used for over a year to calm him when he got overstimulated.

Building from the previous chapter, you have narrowed down five or six areas you are trying to support your child in, start there. Have six areas in the house you are going to use for targeted domains.

Communication

Communication Visuals may not need to do a lot of remodeling, but you would need to do a lot of printing, cut-outs, lamination, and velcro gluing to make laminated cut-out pieces stick. Please see the link to **"How to make a DIY PECS Board at home"** on the resources page.

Set up a central corner accessible to your child, so it's easy for them to reach their PECS tools and indicate needs. A work area close to this central "visuals" spot helps create learning opportunities. Also have visuals in the kitchen, like on the kitchen fridge side door or in front or other areas close to the food, so your child learns where food is actually kept and begins to build some independence.

Create visual schedules for the day. It should be put up in your child's bedroom so it's one of the first things he sees when he wakes up. Daily schedules should show the flow of activities for the day, start with a basic schedule e.g Wakeup, brush, Bath, Breakfast, school, lunch, home, siesta, brush, bath, bedtime, etc, then you can create more specific and detailed ones, e.g class schedules, the addition of time for activities, as your child's understanding of routine grows.

You should also have a visual in the toilet for potty time. It's never too early to start showing your child good toilet and hygiene practices and help them follow the routine as soon as you see them take interest. I began using this free toilet sequencing visual below when my son was 3 years old and he was instantly interested in washing his hands after potty time. He does this independently now.

Communication however expands beyond just visuals, so whatever you decide to employ in your home to meet your set goals in addition to the visuals as outlined in Table 2, ensure you create comfortable spaces and spots within the home to execute your plan.

Motor skills

Now, if you have enough outdoor space, you can create a proprioception corner, the same goes for sensory which is coming up below. Have an area within or outside the home where you can mount a trampoline or therapy swing. However, I completely understand that this may not be possible with limited space. You can have tools that are easy to fold or put away after use, like a crawl tunnel or in-door stepping stones. When you do launch a motor tool watch and support your child use it and ensure he is happy and safe.

For **fine motor skills** have a box where you can store these tools, e.g. pencil grips, play dough, and string toys. Just ensure the box has a lid, as fine motor skill tools tend to be small and can present a choking hazard.

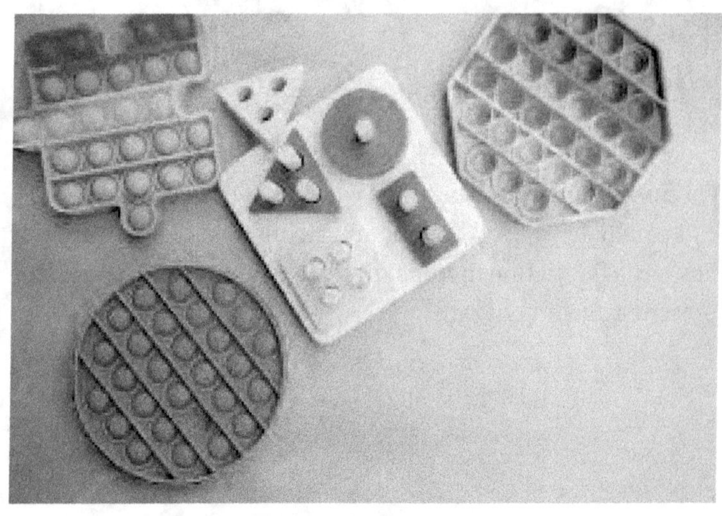

Molding clay is highly recommended as a start tool to build fine motor skills and strengthen the wrist muscles. My son had a hard time writing with a pencil because of his weak wrist, when he started using molding clay, he began to create shapes at first, then words and letters, soon logo's became his main thing, and it's now a great past time and hobby for him. He can sit for hours creating and recreating company logos. Warning though, your child may not like the texture, try a couple of different ones as they vary in consistency, support your child in use, and demonstrate the making of shapes, see where this takes you both. We are headed somewhere pretty awesome!

Sensory

Create a sensory corner, this is one of my favorite home-proofing enhancements. I have a pretty small apartment, so I've had to be pretty creative with the corner I use. I started with having weighted blankets and jackets and a few sensory toys and balls in a box. Since then, I've screwed up a sensory board and added Visual Calmers to the corner. When I have a bigger space, a bean chair is in the works. Choose a space and kit it with sensory relievers for your child. This corner will become your child's and your best spot to calm down when a meltdown is brewing or already in full onslaught! You can also put up visuals of calming techniques in this corner and practice them with your child. Again it is never too early to begin practicing calming techniques with your child. I especially like the calming technique visuals that show the cycle of a flower(for smell) and Candle (for blow), they work great for us!

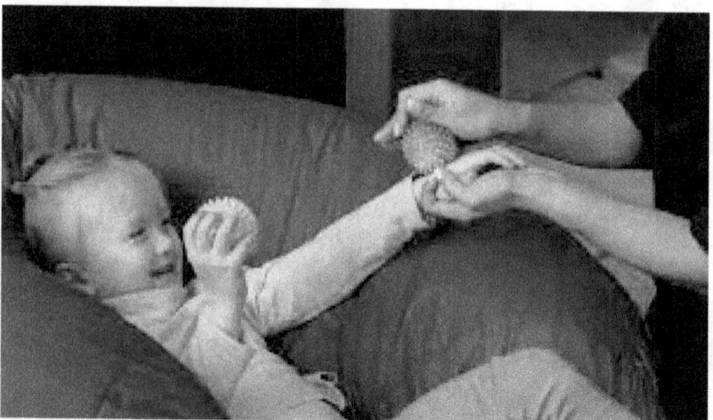

Cognition

These learning tools can share the same central workspace area (desk and chair) with communication, just ensure you keep the education tools and aids in a separate folder or box. This will help you be deliberate about allocating time for communication and time for academic learning. For academics, you'd need whatever is age-appropriate, as mentioned earlier I would always search my son's age milestones and gather resources based on the milestones he should have attained. When he started school I'd go one age up and begin introducing him to the concepts earlier. This way he wouldn't struggle as much in school especially when he moved classes, this has helped him a lot! Now, I request the school curriculum ahead of time and create many lessons from this in visual form, we have a blast going through these during study time, it's made learning at school more bearable. I have also been blessed with a school that's quite supportive and open to inclusion concepts so I'm also "school-proofing" at the moment - that's another book in the making! But back to this subject at hand, a workspace is also important to put up instruction visuals for learning like - a sit at a desk and work visual, study time visuals, etc

Sitting still to work is good practice for your child, it builds pertinent skills for learning in most low and middle-income country classrooms. Even though a lot of schools in high-income countries are flexible about learning and movement, Low and Middle-income countries (LMICs) still operate rigid classroom structures. Your child may resist a restricted workspace at first, as we know children with Autism love to move! So introduce a learning space where your child can sit preferably facing you and include a timer in the mix, giving a reward the longer he succeeds in sitting. The timer bell will also ease the transition from one activity to the other. The timer should be set up on the wall in your child's direct view but away from his direct reach to tamper with.

If you tend to use electronic devices for education, speech, and other learning purposes, the tendency for your child to begin exploring, finding, and using other video-sharing and gaming apps for their learning and entertainment is very high, be sure to use apps to help monitor and limit screen time. The American Academy of Physicians recommends no screen time for children under 2 years, and 1 hour a day for children 2- 12 years of age, while these recommendations may not be realistic in this age of computer gadgets, busy work schedules, and limited caregiver help, it does go to show how overexposed kids are to electronic media.

High volumes of screen time expose children to the dangers of online predators, unhealthy content, hyperstimulation, social seclusion, anxiety, and sleep problems. For children with autism, unlimited screen time means a further negative impact on their social skills and overstimulation of their senses which may lead to meltdowns and longer-term mental health issues like anxiety and sleep disorders.

Limiting screen time is easier said than done, it's something I constantly struggle with, I have deadlines at work, house chores, and limited help. I however have installed a parental control app that locks my son from video sharing and gaming apps after 3 hours, he still has access to educational apps and TV but he tends to get on with other pastimes like molding clay or painting when his device timeout of video streaming and gaming apps. I also try to involve him in the home chores, like tonight we made a pizza together with his younger sister. This was a good 2 hours plus spent interacting, I truly wish we could do this more often! When it comes to screen time, try your best, regularly check what content your child is viewing and searching online, and always remain conscious and cautious of the hazards of too much screen time. Several apps can help you control screen time. Check the resources page for an article to guide your choice. Some apps simply lock the device screens, and others provide feedback on sites visited, time spent on each app used, and even text exchange with a friend across social media and gaming platforms,

Physical Health

I can't overemphasize the importance of having a well-kitted first aid box and a stocked medicine cabinet. All children fall ill, especially under the age of five. For a child with autism, this happens often mainly due to their picky eating habits and poor gut health which has been scientifically linked to lower immunity. For these reasons, you'd be wise to have a stable health insurance plan and basic First Aid medications for fever, cuts, bruises, diarrhea, constipation, and skin breakouts at home. Draw up a simple medical emergency plan in case of sudden accidents with emergency numbers, primary care hospital, route to the hospital, and emergency contacts - this should be written and pasted up in your medical space, well in sight, and family members informed. Meet with the family to review emergency plans and have practice drills so everyone is prepared. You also need appointment reminders for your child's follow-up appointments with their doctor and other therapists

Finally, create a storage box for tools that are no longer useful, outgrown, or never used. Do not throw these items away just yet. Your child may require them for another purpose, begin to use them, or another sibling or child in the community may have use of them.

BUILDING - Advice Summary:

1. Home proofing involves quite a bit of remodeling, so be prepared to lose some ambiance
2. Create spaces for all the domains, don't worry if one domain filters into another, it's supposed to
3. Use visuals across all the domains
4. Keep a storage box to store items that are no longer useful, they may become useful in the future for your child or someone else in your community
5. Screen timers on electronic devices ensure your child is not over-exposed to negative media

7

Embracing the new normal

Creating a Support system

The home team is very important in your home-proofing success. You need everyone at home especially siblings to be aligned with home-proofing plans, and have age-appropriate knowledge of their sibling's diagnosis, and why there need to be some changes. Your home team members are your helpers, from supporting you with learning times, helping to clean up afterward, maintaining spaces and tools, and modeling behaviors and skills. Your home team should have your back at all times. The best way to get this support is to carry them all along from the start. Let them know the changes you will be making and why. Get their input on where to locate what and involve them in the research and in learning how to apply and use the tools with their sibling. There will surely be minor battles for territories within the house, but you all will be able to work something out amicably in the end.

The other sibling(s)

It is also natural for the neurotypical sibling to feel jealous at certain times due to the seemingly greater attention being paid to their autistic sibling. I did experience some defiant and attention-seeking behavior from my daughter early on as a result of the skewed attention to her brother, but I quickly got wind of the situation and corrected my behavior. I had to work to convince her that she was just as special as her brother and I loved her the same as I did him. Make sure to be conscious of this to quickly spot negative energies from siblings. Taking love and time to address the situation, always show appreciation, akin to the appreciation and praise you give their autistic sibling. Have special hang-out times, and let them know that the time is for just you and them. Give them credit for their time working with you on home proofing, and for being loving and responsible for their brother or sister. It's a difficult balance to maintain, but just as you stay mindful of several things I've highlighted earlier, be very mindful of this.

There was also some minimal resistance from my spouse in the course of home proofing, which I still subtly experience as I make more changes and upgrades, however, I caution myself not to go overboard lest my home begin to transform into a special service center of sorts! Whatever you do, please work to maintain communication and peace with your spouse. There is always room for compromise, try to meet each other halfway if disputes do arise, however on some absolute necessities put and keep your foot down.

Finding balance

You must find balance in life amidst home-proofing, long to-do lists, doctor appointments, school runs, homework, therapy, house chores, occupation, and relationships. I cannot tell you how to do this because my situation is quite different from yours and everyone's from every other person's. I can only share how I try to get a balanced mind, body, and spirit. Oftentimes than not, I am unsuccessful, and I feel close to breaking down, yet I push a little harder and try to find balance again, this is the story of my life and I know the story of many Parents of Autistic children.

Try to get enough sleep, I tend to do an average of 5-7 hours, 8 hours on some weekends if I'm lucky. I've installed a sleep time app on my phone to remind me it's time to shut my eyes, I dim the lights, I think happy thoughts...

Eat well. Incorporate fruit and vegetables in your diet, avoid high-sugar foods, and opt for fiber-containing carbs like wheat and oat variants.

Stop smoking and limit alcohol intake. A glass of wine in the evenings is relaxing for me, I do not socialize as often as in my thirties so binge drinking has been out the window for years - this is good for me. Be kind to your body, you need it to last a very long time for yourself and your child.

Exercise, we all know its benefits so I won't spend a lot of time here, I have danced between yoga and Taekwondo for years, I think Taekwondo finally won out, but sometimes I fall in love with a new yoga app and get on that grind again. Movement is important, movement of the body means calmness of mind and spirit. Involve your children in exercising, you want them to form this habit early on. For autistic children, exercise presents opportunities for physical interactions, enhances moods, helps reduce hyperactivity, and improves health, muscle tone, and balance. Meditation and prayers are also cleansing rituals that can help you regain focus and remain grounded.

Celebrating victories

There will be good days, bad days, and absolutely GREAT days! Celebrate your child with praise and positive reinforcers, every time they succeed. This is an absolute rule of thumb because they need these cues to understand they've done the right thing, this is how they learn appropriate behavior, appropriate responses, and appropriate etiquette. You should also be very proud of yourself as a parent and celebrate whenever they hit or exceed a milestone, you should pat yourself on the back often! Celebrate by telling a loved one of the success, or take yourself for a treat!

Celebrate victories, record them, and refer back to them because that's one of the things that will keep you motivated and grounded in your mission. When your child hits a milestone, celebrate it in a small or huge way.

I recall the day my son walked up to me, hugged me, and said "I love you mummy!" Oh! Nothing in this world can describe what an awesome feeling that was! I recall hugging him back furiously and being just short of tears! I called my closest friend and sibling immediately to share the news! That day I could barely wait for my spouse to come home to share this breakthrough! It was all so wonderful! it fuelled my hope, I saw the effort being put in was working, he was in there, I had reached him and he was reaching back. Don't worry too much about any dull responses you get from mothers of neurotypical children when you do share, they just can't relate to the depth of your joy, do not let lackluster responses lessen your victory. Celebrate milestones no matter how small or how big, and make sure the whole family is a part of it. If you want to share with the public through social media posts or blogs, your story could encourage someone who's about to give up on a similar situation, Celebrate - It's all for you.

No stress days

Have no stress days, this is for yourself, your child, and other siblings. I work my son very hard, I try to turn every moment into a learning moment. It has become second nature and has helped him a lot - please learn and institute this strategy. However, this can become laborious, and sometimes, I see my son reaching from behind weary eyes screaming "Mom Enough!" So I let him, his sibling, and myself be. We all have the whole day to ourselves doing whatever we please. I take that whole day off and away from the world of Autism, I chill with sugary snacks, wine, and cable TV and I let him and his sister do pretty much what they want. Nowadays, it's him binging on his device, looping videos, bringing his favorite books to life in drawings, and molding logos....while his sister tries to and sometimes succeeds in pulling him out for some imaginative play, between watching her favorite shows and requesting her own rounds of unlimited sweets. It's always a blissful day and a necessary one at that, but we keep it to once or twice every quarter, and that's why they are so special and refreshing. At day's end both my kids are jacked up, one on sweets, the other on videos, it takes a moment to get them to sleep, but it is all so worth it to have a glimpse back into what I was conditioned to believe - the deary, boring, but ever still sweet normal, that I only get to enjoy once in a while. There's so much work to be done, and I can't waste more than a day there...

EMBRACING THE NEW NORMAL - Advice Summary

1. Organize your home team, they are the best support system you can have

2. Find balance - Eat, Exercise, and Pray

3. Celebrate and share victories

4. Have yourself a no-stress day

8

Conclusion

Life after an Autism Diagnosis can be scary, however, it is one of the most fulfilling journeys you will ever embark on in your life. There will be good days and completely horrible days. Remember to **Play - Pause - Delete - and Repeat.**

Play the tape called life each day, the story is always the same, yet different with new lessons and victories within your reach every day.

Pause to recharge when you feel on the verge of a breakdown, take a deep breath and enjoy the things you did before. Teach your children to do the same, it's a healthy habit.

Delete - Let go of the people who try to hold you back with unkind and unhelpful words and attitudes. Stow away resources that are no longer useful or pass them on to others whom you know may need them.

Repeat the tape called life every day. Keep moving, your child is growing, discovering, and understanding, they are reaching you and you are reaching them.

If you found this book helpful, I'd appreciate you leave this book a kind review on Amazon- **https://www.amazon.com/review/create-review?&asin**=B0BBH7ZJ3S

Your review will provide valuable guidance to millions of parents around the world who feel overwhelmed and lost after an Autism Diagnosis.

Thank you!

9

Resources

Coping with Grief and Loss - HelpGuide.org. (n.d.). Retrieved August 21, 2022, from https://www.helpguide.org/articles/grief/coping-with-grief-and-loss.htm

Welcome To Holland — Emily Perl Kingsley. (n.d.). Retrieved August 21, 2022, from
https://www.emilyperlkingsley.com/welcome-to-holland

Powerful Ways to Reconnect With Your Child - The Deliberate Mom. (n.d.). Retrieved August 21, 2022, from https://thedeliberatemom.com/reconnect-with-your-child/

Reconnecting with a child – Conscious Creative Courageous Living with Children. (n.d.). Retrieved August 21, 2022, from https://www.creativelivingwithchildren.com/help-for-challenging-times/reconnecting-with-a-child/

Autism & Cognitive Development – BabySparks. (n.d.). Retrieved August 21, 2022, from https://babysparks.com/2019/08/30/aut

ism-cognitive-development/

Children's Developmental Centre. The Nigerian experience. Retrieved August 21, 2022 from https://somope.online/

Gilmour, M. F. (2015). Comparing the Teaching Efficacy of Two Video Modeling Programs Delivered in a Group Format in Special Education Classrooms to Improve Expressive Language. *Journal of Special Education Technology, 30*(2), 112–121. https://doi.org/10.1177/0162643415617377

Proprioception Toys & Tools | The Sensory Spectrum. (n.d.). Retrieved August 21, 2022, from http://www.thesensoryspectrum.com/proprioception-toys-tools/

Meraki Lane. (n.d.). *55 Sensory Room Equipment Essentials for Kids with Autism and SPD.* Retrieved August 21, 2022, from https://www.merakilane.com/55-sensory-room-equipment-essentials-for-kids-with-autism-and-spd/

Autism spectrum disorder and digestive symptoms - Mayo Clinic. (n.d.). Retrieved August 21, 2022, from https://www.mayoclinic.org/diseases-conditions/autism-spectrum-disorder/expert-answers/autism-and-digestive-symptoms/faq-20322778

High Scope. (n.d.). *5 Tools to Help Children Access Emotions | The Playground - Adapted from "Managing Conflict Resolution With Children of Trauma" by Carly Li.* Retrieved August 21, 2022, from https://highscope.org/five-tools-to-help-children-access-emotions/

Whitney Loring, Mary Hamilton. Visual Supports and Autism, Autism speaks, Accessed August 21st 2022 https://www.autism speaks.org/sites/default/files/2018-08/Visual%20Supports%20Tool%20Kit.pdf

Fleischmann, Arthur., & Fleischmann, C. (2012). *Carly's voice: breaking through autism.* 391.

Ladysnessa, L. (2019, December 15). *Book Review: How Can I Talk if My Lips Don't Move?* NeuroClastic. Retrieved August 22, 2022, from https://neuroclastic.com/book-review-how-can-i-talk-if-my-lips-dont-move/#:%7E:text=functioning%20and%20intellect.-,How%20Can%20I%20Talk%20if%20My%20Lips%20Don't%20Move,world%20through%20Tito's%20unique%20perceptions.

Research Shows Three Distinct Thought Styles In People With Autism. (n.d.). Retrieved August 21, 2022, from https://www.forbes.com/sites/quora/2017/07/05/research-shows-three-distinct-thought-styles-in-people-with-autism/?sh=21000bf4221e

How to Make a DIY PECS Board at Home - Normal life Inc. (n.d.). Retrieved August 21, 2022, from https://normallifeinc.com/autism-awareness-blog/how-to-make-a-diy-pecs-board-at-home/

Life, N. (2022, March 18). *How to Make a DIY PECS Board at Home - Normal life Inc.* Normal Life Inc. - Helping Families with Special Needs. Retrieved August 21, 2022, from https://normallifeinc.com/autism-awareness-blog/how-to-make-a-diy-pecs-boa

rd-at-home/

Autism Little Learners - Autism Speech Therapist. (n.d.). Retrieved August 21, 2022, from https://autismlittlelearners.com/

Lauren Pardee. (2022, April 15). *7 Best Parental Control Apps to Monitor and Limit Screen Time.* https://www.parents.com/kids/safety/internet/best-apps-for-parents-to-monitor-and-limit-screen-time/

Brian's creative studio | Facebook. (n.d.). Retrieved August 21, 2022, from https://www.facebook.com/profile.php?id=100063476123869

Julie Hornok. (2021, October 13). *The Best Ways to Support Siblings of Autistic Children - Autism Parenting Magazine.* https://www.autismparentingmagazine.com/autism-siblings-support/

About the Author

Dr Matilda Kerry is a specialist public health doctor who writes both fictional and academic books. She is co-host of "The Doctors Nigeria" TV show and uses her influence to bring awareness to disability inclusion and women's health issues. She is a proud Autism Mum and lives in Lagos - Nigeria with her spouse and two wonderful kids.

Did you find this book helpful? Please click the link below to leave a kind review. Thank you.

https://www.amazon.com/review/create-review?&asin =B0BBH7ZJ3S

You can connect with me on:

https://www.instagram.com/matildakerry360

https://www.amazon.com/review/create-review?&asin=B0BBH7ZJ3S

Also by Matilda Kerry

"Social Skills For Teens" is a crucial guide for teenagers and their parents, offering strategies to build self-confidence and self-esteem. It addresses common social challenges, providing practical advice to foster genuine connections and improve parent-teen relationships. The book covers topics from breaking free from cliques to turning identity crises into growth opportunities, making it a valuable resource for both teens and parents.

Social Skills for Teens

This book supports all teenagers in making friends and being confident in social circles. It is cleverly written to help teens draw from their parent's wealth of knowledge and enjoy their support in navigating the intricacies of socializing without conflict. Contains fun Parent-Teen exercises to grow mutual understanding and respect.